I THINK
I THOUGHT
AND OTHER TRICKY VERBS

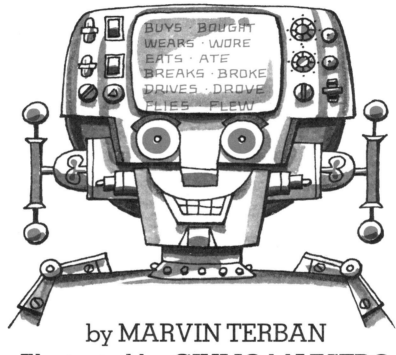

BUYS · BOUGHT
WEARS · WORE
EATS · ATE
BREAKS · BROKE
DRIVES · DROVE
FLIES · FLEW

by MARVIN TERBAN
Illustrated by GIULIO MAESTRO

CLARION BOOKS

Ticknor & Fields: A Houghton Mifflin Company

New York

For David—

David **is** a wonderful son.

His father **was** certain from day number one.

Clarion Books
Ticknor & Fields, a Houghton Mifflin Company

Text copyright ©1984 by Marvin Terban
Illustrations copyright ©1984 by Giulio Maestro

Library of Congress Cataloging in Publication Data

Terban, Marvin.
I think I thought.
Summary: In humorous, alliterative, rhyming couplets,
the present and past tenses of thirty irregular verbs
are presented.
1. English language—Verb—Juvenile literature.
[1. English language—Verb] I. Maestro, Giulio, ill.
II. Title.
PE1273.T4 1984   428.2   83-19034
RNF ISBN 0-89919-231-9   PAP ISBN 0-89919-290-4
V 10 9 8 7 6 5 4 3 2 1

Irregular Verbs

English is a tricky language. Take verbs, for instance. Those are words that tell what someone does or did.

When something is happening right now, we call it the present tense.

I dance.

When something already happened, we call it the past tense.

I danced.

Most verbs are regular. They add "ed" or "d" when they change from the present tense to the past tense.

He looks.   He looked.

We skate.   We skated.

But some verbs are irregular. They don't follow this rule. They change their spelling from the present to the past tense.

They go.   They went.

The tongue-twisting rhymes in this book will help you become familiar with these tricky irregular verbs.

Thelma **thinks** of thrilling things to do.

Thackeray **thought** he knew who threw the shoe.

Baboon **buys** bananas by the bunch.

Boas **bought** baloney for their lunch.

Wendy **wears** her warmest winter woolies.

Willy **wore** a wig to fool the bullies.

Elephant **eats** eight éclairs with her tea.

Alligator **ate** enough for two or three.

Bronco **breaks** branches, briars, and brambles.

Brontosaurus **broke** the bridge into a shambles.

Dromedary **drives** a dump truck in the zoo.

Drake **drove** a car that wasn't new.

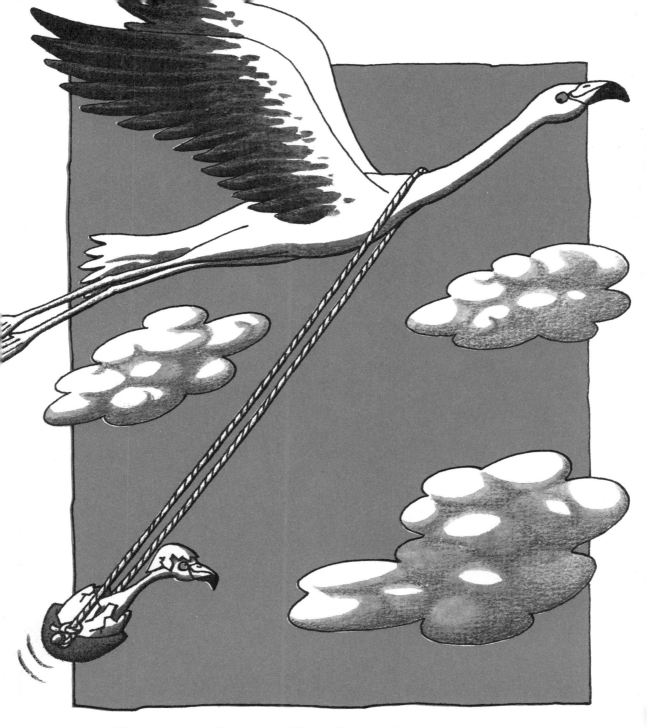

Flamingo **flies** to Florida with her daughter.

Flying Fish **flew** right out of the water.

Tina **teaches** turtles not to stumble.

Talbot **taught** tigers to toss and tumble.

Stingray **sings** songs to submarines.

Sawfish **sang** softly to sardines.

Gorilla **gives** garbage to the goat.

Gibbon **gave** his granny a gorgeous coat.

Belinda **blows** bubbles from bassoons.

Blake **blew** bundles of balloons.

Gwendolyn **gets** galoshes when it rains.

Gregory **got** ghastly headache pains.

Rusty **runs** barefoot in the fountain.

Ramona **ran** a race around the mountain.

Charlie **chooses** chowder, not chop suey.

Chiquita **chose** cheesecake that was gooey.

Celia Seagull **sees** sailors in the sea.

Simon Salmon **saw** a ghostly jamboree.

Sparrow **speaks** sillily to the Sphinx.

Spoonbill **spoke** while playing tiddlywinks.

Sea Horse **stands** straight and strong.

Starfish **stood**—but not for very long.

Ricky **rides** a rickety robot into town.

Rhoda **rode** her roadster up and down.

Rhino **writes** ridiculous riddles.

Roadrunner **wrote** tunes for funny fiddles.

William **wakes** at half past five each day.

Wilma **woke** and started in to play.

Frederick **freezes** fruit pies in his freezer.

Fritzi **froze** her nose, which didn't please her.

Goose **goes** to greet the king and queen.

Weasel **went** and played his tambourine.

Griffith **grows** rows and rows of grapes.

Gretchen **grew** plants with gruesome shapes.

Hyena **hides** a hamburger in her hat.

Hippo **hid** his hot dog from the cat.

Betty **throws** confetti at Freddy.

Teddy **threw** meatballs and spaghetti.

Bullfrog **brings** a banjo to his bride.

Bulldog **brought** a bear for his to ride.

Swan **swims** and swirls and swishes.

Swine **swam**—and angered all the fishes.

Philip **falls** flat upon the ice.

Felicia **fell** twice, which wasn't nice.

Dragon **draws** a princess in distress.

David **drew** a dragon in a dress.

Tanya **takes** Tarantula to show her teacher.

Tommy **took** Tippy to meet a creature.

Here is an alphabetical list of the principal parts of the verbs featured in this book.

Pages	Present tense	Past tense	Past participle
24, 25	blow	blew	blown
12, 13	break	broke	broken
54, 55	bring	brought	brought
6, 7	buy	bought	bought
30, 31	choose	chose	chosen
60, 61	draw	drew	drawn
14, 15	drive	drove	driven
10, 11	eat	ate	eaten
58, 59	fall	fell	fallen
16, 17	fly	flew	flown
26, 27	get	got	gotten
22, 23	give	gave	given
46, 47	go	went	gone
48, 49	grow	grew	grown
50, 51	hide	hid	hidden
38, 39	ride	rode	ridden
28, 29	run	ran	run
32, 33	see	saw	seen
20, 21	sing	sang	sung
34, 35	speak	spoke	spoken
36, 37	stand	stood	stood
56, 57	swim	swam	swum
62, 63	take	took	taken
18, 19	teach	taught	taught
4, 5	think	thought	thought
52, 53	throw	threw	thrown
42, 43	wake	woke or waked	waked or woken
8, 9	wear	wore	worn
40, 41	write	wrote	written